Ch

C000201019

Restaurants

The Food Enthusiast's Long Weekend Guide

Andrew Delaplaine

Andrew Delaplaine is the Food Enthusiast.
When he's not playing tennis,
he dines anonymously
at the Publisher's (considerable) expense.

James Cubby – Senior Editor

The Food Enthusiast's Long Weekend Guide

Table of Contents

INTRODUCTION

The historic part of downtown is on a peninsula formed by two rivers, the Ashley and the Cooper, flowing into the Atlantic. It's got much the same geographical layout as Manhattan does, where you have the East and the Hudson Rivers merging at the tip of Manhattan.

But that's the only thing that will remind you of New York. Charleston was captured in the Civil War without much property damage, so the historic part of town has buildings that are hundreds of years old.

Most of the damage they suffered has come from hurricanes, not cannon balls. The current downtown skyline, with practically no tall buildings due to the city's height restriction ordinance, is dominated by church steeples and the stunning Arthur Ravenel cable-stay bridge completed in 2005 over the Cooper River. The city is a major port on the eastern seaboard of the U.S. and a popular destination for domestic and international tourists.

Charles Towne, as it was first called, was established in 1670 by Anthony Ashley Cooper on the west bank of the Ashley River, Charles Towne Landing, a few miles northwest of the present downtown. By 1680, the settlement had grown and moved to its current location on the peninsula.

Around 1690, the English colonists erected a fortification wall around the small settlement to aid in its defense. The wall sheltered the area, in the present French Quarter, from Cumberland Street south to Water Street, from Meeting Street east to East Bay Street. The wall was destroyed around 1720. Cobblestone lanes and one building remain from this Colonial English Walled Town: the **Powder Magazine**, where the town's supply of gunpowder was stored. Remnants of the Colonial wall were found beneath the **Old Exchange Building**.

Charleston was the first city in the U.S. to pass a historical preservation ordinance. Thus, much of the beautiful architecture, from early Colonial, Georgian, Federal, Greek Revival, and Italianate to Victorian, remains for future generations to see and enjoy.

Charleston is also known as the Holy City due to the numerous church steeples poking out of the low-rise skyline. Another reason: it was one of the few places in the original 13 colonies to provide religious tolerance to the French Huguenots as well as to Jews.

GETTING ABOUT

BY FOOT
Once you're in the historic district, you won't need a car. If the walking is too much for you, hop aboard the DASH shuttles to move between sights on your list. You'll see the signs, but if you want more information, go to www.ridecarta.com

CHARLESTON BLACK CAB COMPANY
843-216-2627
www.charlestonblackcabcompany.com
They have roomy London-style taxis from the airport to downtown. If you're going to hire a car and driver

while here, get one of these. Much more comfortable than regular cars. Use them to go to the plantations outside town.

GRAY TOURS
See listing under What To See & Do.

TOURS
There are many walking tours, which give you the opportunity to see more than just driving past in a bus or carriage. There is a walking tour for virtually every interest. You will find Pub Tours, Civil War tours, culinary tours, ghost tours, Gulla tours, architecture tours, art tours, and even pirate tours. Some of the walking tour companies offer tours with guides in period costume. Charleston Pirate Tours even has a costumed guide whose parrot, a blue and gold macaw, accompanies the tour.

BROAD STREET
In the historic district, there is a major east-west street, Broad Street, which divides two areas in historic downtown, aptly named *North of Broad* and *South of Broad*. Those South of Broad were nicknamed SOBs, and those Slightly North of Broad were SNOBs. The *French Quarter*, founded by the French Huguenots, is just south of the Market Area along the waterfront. The area near the southern tip of the peninsula, where the Ashley and Cooper Rivers meet, is known as *The Battery*.

The A to Z Listings

Ridiculously Extravagant
Sensible Alternatives
Quality Bargain Spots

The culinary world was upended when for three years running, a restaurant from Charleston took high honors when it snagged the prestigious James Beard Award for Best Southeastern Chef (**Hominy Grill** took the honors first, followed by **Fig**, then **McCrady's**). Things have never been the same since.

That being said, the one meal you must have to get the feeling of old Charleston is a Lowcountry Oyster Roast. They do them all year-round at **<u>Bowens Island</u>** (see listing below). You eat roasted oysters and huge hushpuppies and you'll never be happier. Bowens is on stilts over the marsh. The oysters (they call them "cluster oysters") come directly from the water and are steamed open on metal sheets over a

11

brick-lined pit. A wood fire is important because the smoke is essential to create the unforgettable taste. All you need is lemon to finish them off when they are laid out before you. (Some like Tabasco.) Beer is the drink of choice.

Let's talk Fried Chicken, shall we? You'll see it on every menu. In "The Virginia House-Wife" by Mary Randolph, published in 1824, you'll find the first recipe for Southern Fried Chicken: "Cut [the chicken] up as for the fricassee, dredge the pieces well with flour, sprinkle them with salt, put them into a good quantity of boiling lard, and fry them a light brown."

Can't get much simpler than that. And yet such simplicity has allowed the term "fried chicken" to be interpreted in hundreds of thousands of different ways, almost all of them perfectly wonderful, to my mind, having been raised in South Carolina on a plantation. With slaves adding spices redolent of their West African homeland, the variations on the theme exploded, and continue to unfold today. Even in the finest of fine restaurants, you'll find world-renowned chefs unable to shake the urge to put their signature touch to this most American of all-American foods.

167 RAW
289 E Bay St, Charleston, 843-579-4997
www.167raw.com
CUISINE: Seafood/Seafood Market
DRINKS: Beer & Wine Only
SERVING: Lunch & Dinner; closed Sun
PRICE RANGE: $$
NEIGHBORHOOD: Ansonborough

Casual seafood eatery popular with locals and tourists. It's got an ultra-casual atmosphere, with menu items scribbled on a mirror. Framed fishing guides hang on the white-tiled walls. Seafood selections include oysters, lobster rolls, fish tacos, shrimp tacos, and ceviche. Favorites: Tuna Burger and Lobster roll. Nice wine list. Usually a line, so be prepared to wait.

BERTHA'S KITCHEN
2332 Meeting St Rd, North Charleston, 843-554-6519
http://runinout.com/Bertha
CUISINE: Southern; soul food
DRINKS: No Booze
SERVING: Lunch & Dinner
PRICE RANGE: $
Up on the less fashionable northern end of Meeting Street you'll find Bertha's. Perfectly executed soul food. Fried pork chops, lima beans, mac-n-cheese, okra soup, collard greens, yams, baked chicken (a

dish often ignored by tourists who don't know how good it can be), stew beef.

BOWENS ISLAND RESTAURANT
1870 Bowens Island Rd, Charleston, 843-795-2757
www.bowensisland.biz
CUISINE: Seafood; oyster roast
DRINKS: Full Bar
SERVING: Dinner; closed Sun & Mon
PRICE RANGE: $$$
A local seafood institution that offers counter service, a bar, waterfront views, and authentic seafood dishes.

Favorites include: Fresh oysters, Fried Chicken Breast strips and Crab cakes. This no-frills two-level eatery is a favorite of locals and tourists. Customers had scrawled graffiti on every inch of its walls. But when it reopened atop 18-foot stilts, it boasted a much better view and a superior screened in deck overlooking Folly Creek. Spend time reading all the new graffiti (or add some of your own) while you wait for the roasted oysters. Always crowded. Always worth it.

BUTCHER & BEE
1085 Morrison Dr, Charleston, 843-619-0202
www.butcherandbee.com
CUISINE: Sandwiches
DRINKS: No Booze; BYOB
SERVING: Lunch & Dinner
PRICE RANGE: $$
Popular eatery known for their fresh creative sandwiches. (They even make the bread for the famous **McCrady's**.) Great place for a casual brunch. The French toast is tasty and they make a delicious baked egg and tomato with tahini. There's an herb garden out back. Each sandwich is like a work of art. It's open late and attracts a lot of chefs after their own restaurants have closed for the night. BYOB.

CANNON GREEN
103 Spring St, Charleston, 843-817-6299
www.cannongreencharleston.com
CUISINE: Mediterranean
DRINKS: Full Bar

SERVING: Dinner Tues- Sat; Lunch on Sun; Closed on Mon
PRICE RANGE: $$$
NEIGHBORHOOD: Cannonborough
Executive Chef Amalia Scatena (who trained in Italy) offers an a la carte menu of seasonal Mediterranean fare. Menu picks: Cioppino (the best in the whole state, I'm sure), Raviolo and Shrimp & Grits. Elegant eatery, popular choice for weddings, the restaurant serves innovative cocktails and has an impressive wine list. Great choice for Sunday Brunch. Reservations recommended.

CAVIAR AND BANANAS
College of Charleston
51 George St, Charleston, 843-577-7757
www.caviarandbananas.com
CUISINE: Breakfast/Sandwiches
DRINKS: Beer & Wine Only
SERVING: Breakfast, Lunch & Dinner (closes at 8 p.m.)
PRICE RANGE: $$
A combination gourmet market and café offering a bountiful menu of sandwiches, salads, sushi, and treats like their Duck Confit Panini. Great spot for breakfast or to collect items for a picnic.

CHARLESTON GRILL
224 King St, Charleston, 843-577-4522
www.charlestongrill.com
CUISINE: American
DRINKS: Full Bar
SERVING: Dinner
PRICE RANGE: $$$$
A grand ballroom of a restaurant tucked away in a posh hotel. From a glamorous banquette, you can take in the sophisticated tunes of the Quentin Baxter Ensemble and the very polite antics of practically all of Charleston, from dads and debutantes to Gullah painters. Snack on the truffle parmesan popcorn and a kiwi version of the Pimm's Cup. General Manager Mickey Bakst and his staff have carefully created an ambiance that is all at once mellow and lively, traditional and contemporary. Soft jazz bounces off of wood-paneled walls and crisp, white tablecloths. Servers trained in the French tradition delight guests

with each menu suggestion and wine pairing. Seamless service, orchestrated by the attentive, knowledgeable and approachable staff, sets the stage for an unforgettable dining experience.

CHEZ NOUS
6 Payne Ct, Charleston, 843-579-3060
www.cheznouschs.com
CUISINE: French
DRINKS: Beer & Wine Only
SERVING: Lunch & Dinner; closed Mon.
PRICE RANGE: $$$
NEIGHBORHOOD: Cannonborough
Small neighborhood eatery with a daily-changing international menu with just two appetizers, 2 entrees and 2 desserts. Payne Street is not a touristy area, and the restaurant is housed in a classic two-story house, so you'll feel like you're eating in someone's home. Nice selection of French wines.

CHUBBY FISH
252 Coming St, 854-222-3949
www.chubbyfishcharleston.com
CUISINE: Seafood/Tapas
DRINKS: Full Bar
SERVING: Dinner, Closed Sun & Mon.
PRICE RANGE: $$$
NEIGHBORHOOD: Downtown / Cannonborough
Ultra-simple small neighborhood eatery featuring creative seafood-focused menu all written out for you on a blackboard (that's raised above the open kitchen) listing raw bar items, whole fish available that day, small plates and large plates. Oysters from the

Carolinas and other Southern states are featured. Favorites: Smoked Bluefish with curry rice; roasted bone marrow with crispy rock shrimp; Grouper Cheeks with chive butter; Chicken-fried swordfish collar. For a treat try the tempura-battered frog legs. But beware that the menu changes with whatever's fresh, fresh, fresh. That said, you can't go wrong here. Impressive wine list and wine pairings for such a tiny establishment.

CIRCA 1886
149 Wentworth St., 843-853-7828
www.circa1886.com
CUISINE: American

DRINKS: Full bar
SERVING: Mon - Sat, dinner from 5:30, closed Sun; a little dressy; no shorts, etc.
PRICE RANGE: $$$$

Chef Marc Collins is the star here, and he allows influences from around the world to help him forge the unusual Lowcountry food he serves here. Think less butter and less fat. Think whole grains. Menu is decidedly and intentional very seasonal in keeping with the craze that has engulfed Charleston in recent years. Grilled quail with a spicy plum sauce and smoked cheddar grits; hearts of palm in a passion fruit vinaigrette; pork shoulder with "coffee essence," mustard greens and a sour orange hollandaise; lamb served with sweet potato celery root and cauliflower gremolata; wild mushroom pot pie. Don't ignore Pastry Chef Lovorn's delicacies: peaches & cream soufflé, strawberry shortcake (we were there in August when the fruit was perfect). This place is so good it makes you want to move here permanently.

COAST
39 D John St, Charleston, 843-722-8838
www.coastbarandgrill.com
CUISINE: Seafood, Cajun & Creole
DRINKS: Full Bar
SERVING: Dinner
PRICE RANGE: $$

A casual, hip restaurant in a former indigo warehouse. (Quick—do you know what indigo is?) It has open oak grills and tin-roofed booths that draw savvy locals. The menu, which specializes in local seafood, has a Creole twist.

THE CODFATHER, PROPER FISH & CHIPS

4254 Spruill Ave, 843-789-4649
No Website
CUISINE: Fish & Chips, Seafood
DRINKS: Beer & Wine
SERVING: Lunch & Dinner, Closed Sun & Mon.
PRICE RANGE: $$
NEIGHBORHOOD: North Charleston
Known as the only place in town to get proper fish
and chips made the traditional British way. Fish is
always nice and crisp, malt vinegar, the works. (They
even serve those mushy peas you get in England, only
they're better here.) Also, fresh baked British style
meat pies and sausage rolls. Nice selection of draft
beer from the old country. Bare bones interior with a
mural on the wall that tries its damnedest to provide a
little "atmosphere," but it's the fish & chips you want.
A few picnic tables under umbrellas outside, if you
like.

DARLING OYSTER BAR

513 King St, 843-641-0821
www.thedarling.com
CUISINE: Seafood/Raw Bar
DRINKS: Full Bar
SERVING: Dinner, Late night
PRICE RANGE: $$
NEIGHBORHOOD: Radcliffeborough
Trendy eatery in a century-old building with high
ceilings, tall windows looking out into the street, a
busy vibe, white-tiled floors and a beautiful long bar
where you can get counter service for the Darling's

creative seafood-focused menu or just have drinks. Tables along the side and in the back provide a lower-key, more private experience. Super place I really loved. Favorites: Raw oysters; Baked oysters with bacon; Shrimp & Grits with Cheddar, country ham and fennel; Fried fish baskets. Get a side order of the hush puppies with sorghum butter. Daily seafood specials. Oyster shooters are a must—just to get you started.

DAVE's CARRY-OUT
42 Morris St., Charleston, 843-577-7943
No Website
CUISINE: Seafood; soul food
DRINKS: Full Bar
SERVING: Lunch (11-3), dinner (5-11); closed Sunday
PRICE RANGE: $
I always find it amusing that people will go to **McCrady's** and **Husk** and pay a New York dollar for what is really just tarted up Southern cuisine you can

get at lots of places without all the fuss and white tablecloths. No one fries shrimp this—what's the word?—*lightly*. It's just enough batter and then it's like they flash fry the shrimp. Whole fried flounder, fish sandwich, all the side dishes are good. Pure excellence. (Call ahead before you make a special trip—they sometimes close without any notice. They just lock the door and leave. Maybe they go shrimping. Whenever I ask, they just shrug.)

EARLY BIRD DINER
1644 Savannah Hwy, Charleston, 843-277-2353
www.earlybirddiner.com
CUISINE: American
DRINKS: No Booze
SERVING: Breakfast, Lunch & Dinner
PRICE RANGE: $
A funky diner inspired eatery filled with art with a menu of American diner classics. The excellent coffee comes from a local roaster, King Bean. Staff here are blunt, no frills, to the point. A big locals' hangout. Menu favorites include: Fried chicken with mushroom gravy and Fettuccine with vegetables. Great selection of desserts that changes daily.

EDMUND'S OAST
1081 Morrison Dr, Charleston. 843-727-1145
www.edmundsoast.com
CUISINE: Gastropub
DRINKS: Full Bar
SERVING: Dinner nightly
PRICE RANGE: $$

Find out why this spot was included on the 100 Best Southern Restaurants list. A hip e`atery with a creative menu of American favorites. Great brunch destination. Bar features four dozen beers on tap including several house beers. The beers go just fine with their homemade pickled shrimp. Menu favorites include: Lamb meatballs, heritage pumpkin custard, chicken & rice porridge and Chocolate Mousse with caramel.

EVO PIZZERIA & CRAFT BAKERY
1075 E Montague Ave, 843-225-1796
www.evopizza.com
CUISINE: Pizza
DRINKS: Beer & Wine
SERVING: Lunch & Dinner
PRICE RANGE: $$$
NEIGHBORHOOD: North Charleston / Park Circle
Casual eatery in a nondescript red-brick building doesn't do justice to the quality of food served in this place offering wood-fired pizza with recipes that change during the seasons, a nice touch, so you might get a pizza with pumpkin on it during Halloween. Everything is fresh from the mozzarella to the pizza dough. Everything is fresh. Can I say that a third time? Besides offering some 10 pizza selections (Pastrami & Corn; Chorizo & Tomato; Pork Trifecta, for example), they also have great sandwiches, good salads, and starters like Wood-fired olives (so flavorful). Impressive list of beers and ciders. Next door they have a **Craft Bakery** with excellent out-of-this-world sandwiches and dinner specials. I'm getting used to the red brick.

FIG
232 Meeting St, Charleston, 843-805-5900
www.eatatfig.com
CUISINE: American
DRINKS: Full Bar
SERVING: Dinner
PRICE RANGE: $$$

I mentioned earlier that the chef here, **Mike Lata**, is a
James Beard Award winner, so you can expect only
the finest ingredients prepared (and served) expertly.
The menu always has new items on it, but one thing
that's always on the menu—the fish stew en cocotte
(cooked in ramekins). This is a flavorful stew with a
strong scent of saffron in the broth that's simply
divine. In it you'll find white shrimp, squid, mussels,
fingerling potatoes, rouille. Other selections might

include Rebellion Farms suckling pig, clams steamed in capers, flounder dusted in corn flour. The side dishes (order for the table) might be beets, fresh greens, farrotto. Mike usually lists the farms where the food originated, even down to the lettuces. FIG, by the way, stands for "Food Is Good." (Because the food everywhere is *not* always good, I would change that to "Fig Is Good.")

FOLLY BEACH CRAB SHACK
26 Center St, Folly Beach, 843-588-3080
www.crabshacks.com
CUISINE: Seafood/American
DRINKS: Full Bar
SERVING: Lunch & Dinner
PRICE RANGE: $$
A relaxed eatery that offers fresh seafood served with a Southern twist. Favorites include: Crab Shack Famous Deviled Crabs and Smothered Spicy Fried Grouper. 3 locations.

GAULART & MALICLET / FAST & FRENCH
98 Broad St, 843-577-9797

https://fastandfrenchcharleston.com/
CUISINE: French-American
DRINKS: Beer & Wine
SERVING: Breakfast, Lunch & Dinner; Closed Sundays
PRICE RANGE: $$
Small place on Broad with a cozy intimate bar and a communal high-top table is setting for this busy café with a menu mostly of sandwiches, soups and salads. Bar-style seating. Creative French offerings like Turkey and Brie on a French baguette. I always get the daily special, which when I was there was a Hearty Beef Stew with Chèvre, Baguette, Fresh Fruit & a Glass of French Wine, all for one low price. (I also got the soup, which was the Seafood Chowder, though they have 3 or 4 soups to choose from.)

GLASS ONION
1219 Savannah Hwy, Charleston, 843-225-1717
www.ilovetheglassonion.com
CUISINE: Southern
DRINKS: Beer & Wine Only

SERVING: Lunch & Dinner; closed Sun
PRICE RANGE: $$$
Popular upbeat eatery offering a menu of locally sourced Southern fare. Menu picks: Fried quail and Fried NC Trout with Grits and Bacon Braised Turnips. Great desserts like Bread pudding and Crème Brulee. Green wine list.

GOAT SHEEP COW
106 Church St, 843-480-2526
804 Meeting St, 843-203-3118
www.goatsheepcow.com
CUISINE: Cheese & Wine Shop
DRINKS: Wine Bar
SERVING: Lunch & Dinner, Closed Sundays
PRICE RANGE: $$
NEIGHBORHOOD: Downtown
Chic European-style wine bar and cheese shop with old red brick interior, a red leather-style tufted banquette against one wall, a very spacious bar area. Menu with sandwich specials, soups and salads like the Ratatouille Tart, the Chicken Pot Pie, a Daily quiche, charcuterie boards. Fabulous selection of cheeses, of course. Impressive wine list. Patio seating. Wine specials.

GRILL 225
Market Pavilion Hotel
225 E Bay St, Charleston, 843-723-0500
www.grill225.com
CUISINE: Steakhouses
DRINKS: Full Bar
SERVING: Lunch & Dinner

PRICE RANGE: $$$$

One of the best steakhouses in town. It's got the steakhouse "look" down pat. Dark paneled walls rising to a coffered ceiling with impressive moldings, handsome paintings adorning the walls, circular booths against the wall, arched windows looking out into the busy street outside the Market Pavilion Hotel. It's got the usual suspects on the menu, with prices equal to what you'd spend in Miami on South Beach or New York. Any number of cuts of prime steak, Maine lobsters, lots of excellent seafood starters (oysters, scallops, etc.)

THE GROCERY
4 Cannon St, Charleston, 843-302-8825
www.thegrocerycharleston.com
CUISINE: American
DRINKS: Full Bar
SERVING: Dinner; open also for Lunch on Sun, closed Mon
PRICE RANGE: $$$
Comfortable eatery that features Chef Kevin Johnson's seasonal menu made with local and regional ingredients. Favorites include: Warm pear salad, Black Bass, and Roasted Duck Breast. Nice selection of beers and wine. One of the better brunches in town. (I'm a fan of their spicy bloody Mary.)

GULLAH GRUB
877 Sea Island Pkwy, Saint Helena Island, 843-838-3841
www.gullahgrub.com
CUISINE: Seafood/Barbecue
DRINKS: No Booze
SERVING: Lunch & Dinner; Lunch only on Sun, closed Sat
PRICE RANGE: $$
Restaurant with a rustic general store feel offering regional Low Country cuisine. Menu favorites include: Fried Shark Strips with potato salad and BBQ Ribs.

HALL'S CHOPHOUSE
434 King St, 843-727-0090
www.hallschophouse.com
CUISINE: Steakhouse, Seafood
DRINKS: Full Bar
SERVING: Dinner, Lunch & Dinner on Sat & Sun.
PRICE RANGE: $$$$
NEIGHBORHOOD: Radcliffeborough
Red brick walls, white tablecloth service, subdued
lighting, a piano player tinkling away against the far
wall, interesting artwork adorning the walls—all this
sets the scene in this elegant eatery offering a menu of
sizeable cuts of beef and seafood specialties (but stick
with the excellent selection of beef). Favorites: Dry
aged ribeye and Lamb chops Vegetarian options. As a
side, get the cornmeal-fried okra or the pepper jack
creamed corn. Reservations recommended. Sunday
gospel brunch. Has a very lively bar scene, which
gives the place a little more jump than you expect in a
standard steakhouse. Which is very nice. The bar
makes this a great place for lunch. You get the high
quality of fine food in an unstuffy atmosphere.

HANK'S SEAFOOD RESTAURANT
10 Hayne St, Charleston, 843-723-3474
www.hanksseafoodrestaurant.com
CUISINE: Seafood
DRINKS: Full Bar
SERVING: Dinner; open nightly
PRICE RANGE: $$$
Located in a turn-of-the-century warehouse
overlooking the City Market, this very popular
restaurant and bar offers a great selection of seafood

and raw-bar selections. Popular choices include the Seafood a la Wando and Curried Shrimp.

HANNIBAL'S KITCHEN
16 Blake St, 843-722-2256
www.hannibalkitchen.com
CUISINE: Barbecue, American Traditional
DRINKS: No Booze
SERVING: Breakfast, Lunch & Dinner, Closed Sundays
PRICE RANGE: $
NEIGHBORHOOD: East Side
Family-owned eatery known for their Southern seafood specialties in a simple place with no noticeable décor to speak of but also with no pretension. You'll find a lot of places in the Low Country serving shrimp and grits, but the version they have here is one of the best I've encountered. Favorites: Fried chicken with mac & fries; Smothered Liver & Onions; I grew up on fried pork chops and never see them on a menu anymore—here they are wonderful; they have daily specials, and my favorite is the stewed gizzards; Grilled Whiting.

HIGH COTTON
199 E Bay St, Charleston, 843-724-3815
www.highcottoncharleston.com
CUISINE: American, Southern
DRINKS: Full bar
SERVING: Dinner daily, Sat lunch, and Sun brunch
PRICE RANGE: $$$

The dining rooms have heart pine floors and antique brick, a perfect setting for their excellent Southern food.

HUSK
74-76 Queen St, Charleston, 843-577-2500
www.huskrestaurant.com
CUISINE: Southern American, Seafood
DRINKS: Full Bar
SERVING: Lunch & Dinner
PRICE RANGE: $$$
Book a table (weeks in advance) in this elegant 19th Century mansion that is the house that Chef Sean Brock built. It's easier to get a table at lunch, and the Husk Cheeseburger is on the menu. You used to have to order the fried chicken 24 hours ahead, but if not,

get it. It may be the best fried chicken you ever ate. Cornmeal-dusted catfish from N.C., wood-fired clams from nearby McClellanville. But these are just the beginning of the wonders you'll discover at this award-winning eatery. Brock says, "The secret to good food is good dirt and plant varieties," and he has worked long and hard to bring back heritage seeds used to grow the food he serves here. I could go on and on about this guy, but just make this a must-visit on your trip to the Holy City.

JESTINE'S KITCHEN
251 Meeting St, Charleston, 843-722-7224
www.jestineskitchen.com
CUISINE: Southern

DRINKS: No Booze
SERVING: Lunch & Dinner; closed Mondays
PRICE RANGE: $$
This old-school restaurant offers a menu of Southern classics like Fried chicken and Gumbo. Great desserts like Banana Pudding and Coca Cola cake.

KAMINSKY'S MOST EXCELLENT CAFÉ
78 N Market St, Charleston, 843-853-8270
www.kaminskys.com
CUISINE: Desserts
DRINKS: Full Bar
SERVING: Afternoon-Late night
PRICE RANGE: $$,
The desserts here are prepared fresh daily by the talented pasty chefs who offer a new selection every day. Great menu of specialty coffees, milkshakes (some made with brandy or kahlua) and dessert martinis.

LE FARFALLE
15 Beaufain St, 843-212-0920
www.lefarfallecharleston.com
CUISINE: Italian
DRINKS: Full Bar
SERVING: Lunch & Dinner
PRICE RANGE: $$
NEIGHBORHOOD: Harleston Village, Downtown
The white tablecloths add a touch of elegance to what is a pretty bare room with hard wood floors and an industrial style ceiling. Outdoor patio at night especially is a romantic setting under a big tree providing a spacious canopy. Lively bar scene makes this neighborhood eatery quite popular. The raw bar is basic, but covers what you need: good oysters, lump crab meat, a different crudo every night. They offer mostly Italian fare, creatively imagined, expertly prepared. Housemade pastas. Favorites: Octopus Carpaccio; Polpette (pork meatballs alla Siciliana); a good starter would be the Umbian style stewed chickpeas—interesting flavors at work here; the Pork Chop from their Hogs City supplier is done with caramelized fennel; the Veal Chop is smoked in hay, of all things, imparting a singular taste, and the pureed potatoes only add to the flavorful mix; and the Whipped Ricotta. Weekend brunch. Extensive wine list.

LEON'S OYSTER SHOP
LEON'S FINE POULTRY & OYSTERS
698 King St, Charleston, 843-531-6500
www.leonsoystershop.com
CUISINE: Seafood/Southern

DRINKS: Beer & Wine Only
SERVING: Lunch & Dinner
PRICE RANGE: $$$
This locals' hangout in a cleverly reclaimed former
auto body shop downtown offers a creative menu of
Southern fare. The oysters can be had raw, fried,
char-grilled or Rockefeller. The

chef also has "updated Southern picnic sides" like
cole slaw made with yogurt instead of mayo. Other
standouts: Leon's Fried Chicken that is cooked to
order and the Black-eyed pea salad. There's only one
dessert: soft-serve ice cream. The owner, curiously
enough, made his name as a star bartender at **FIG**, but
here he only serves beer & wine.

LEWIS BARBECUE
464 North Nassau St, 843-805-9500
www.lewisbarbecue.com

CUISINE: Barbecue
DRINKS: Full Bar
SERVING: Lunch & Dinner
PRICE RANGE: $$
NEIGHBORHOOD: NoMo
Popular BBQ eatery serving up Texas-style house-smoked meats. Some of the counters are made with reclaimed wood that has a distressed look. The stripped-down look of the place means the emphasis is on the food. I had a look at the HUGE smokers in the back. Very impressive, but what they turn out is even more impressive. Favorites: Prime Beef Brisket and Pulled pork. Daily specials—I was there on a Wednesday when it was a Barbecue Reuben made with pastrami they cured right here in house. Delicious. Counter service. Outdoor seating available.

LITTLE JACK'S TAVERN
710 King St, 843-531-6868
www.littlejackstavern.com
CUISINE: American Traditional
DRINKS: Full Bar
SERVING: Lunch & Dinner
PRICE RANGE: $$
NEIGHBORHOOD: Downtown
Checkered tablecloths set the tone in this classic American tavern offering a menu of steaks, salads & sandwiches. Has a long spacious bar which makes a great place to have lunch. Classic cocktails. If you're new, try the Garlic knots if you don't mind overdoing it on the carbs. The Tavern burger is a big favorite, but I usually opt in for the Brick Chicken (half a

roasted chicken). Has a little crisp to it but lots of flavorful juices.

LOST DOG CAFÉ

106 West Huron Ave, Folly Beach, 843-588-9669
www.lostdogfollybeach.com
CUISINE: American
DRINKS: Full Bar
SERVING: Breakfast & Lunch; open daily
PRICE RANGE: $$
A popular inviting café that serves breakfast all day and a great selection of sandwiches, wraps and salads. Bloody Mary (served in a mason jar) and Folly Eggs Benedict was perfect choice for breakfast.

MAGNOLIAS

185 E Bay St, Charleston, 843-577-7771
www.magnoliascharleston.com
CUISINE: Southern
DRINKS: Full Bar
SERVING: Lunch & Dinner
PRICE RANGE: $$$
CUISINE: Southern
DRINKS: Full bar

SERVING: Mon – Sat lunch, Dinner nightly, and Sun brunch
PRICE RANGE: $$$
Magnolias ignited a culinary renaissance when it opened in 1990, paving the way for countless other restaurants across the South. Today, led by executive chef Donald Drake and his team, Magnolias remains a forerunner in upscale Southern cuisine, blending traditional ingredients and cooking techniques with modern flair for artful presentations.

The soul of the South meets the spark of innovation in dishes such as the Down South Egg Roll stuffed with collard greens, chicken, and Tasso ham, served with red pepper purée, spicy mustard sauce, and peach chutney and Shellfish over Grits with sautéed shrimp, sea scallops, lobster, creamy white grits, lobster butter sauce and fried spinach.

MARTHA LOU'S KITCHEN

1068 Morrison Dr., Charleston, 843-577-9583
www.marthalouskitchen.com
CUISINE: Southern; soul food
DRINKS: No booze
SERVING: Breakfast, lunch (closes at 5)
PRICE RANGE: $

Unpretentious place where Martha Lou Gadsden has
been cooking for decades. If she's not there, her
daughters will be. Excellent fried chicken, but I
always pass it up (too many gourmet cooks around
the country are making some pretty good fried
chicken, so you can get it anywhere) and opt for the
smothered pork chops (a dish those fancy chefs
haven't mastered yet or are too proud to cook), green
beans cooked almost to a delicious mush, or try the
fried whiting over grits. Heavenly food for someone
like me who grew up not far from here. I draw the
line at chitlins (chitterlings), but if you want them,
you can get them here at this gritty, wonderful, iconic
place.

McCRADY'S

155 E. Bay St, 843-577-0025
www.mccradysrestaurant.com
CUISINE: American
DRINKS: Full bar
SERVING: Dinner daily
PRICE RANGE: $$$$

McCrady's Restaurant, which is listed on the National
Register of Historic Places and Landmarks, represents
the best of the amalgam that is new Southern fine

dining, serving as a canvas for postmodern gastronomy. The menu, created by Chef Sean Brock, 2010 James Beard Best Chef Southeast award-winner, centers around inventive cuisine fresh from the farm and local purveyors. McCrady's bar specializes in hand-crafted cocktails and features a Wine Spectator Award-winning wine list, as well as a diverse and delicious Bar Snack menu created by Chef Brock. Each day, a chalkboard above the bar offers several featured snacks

MERCANTILE AND MASH
701 E Bay St, Charleston, 843-793-2636
www.mercandmash.com
CUISINE: American (Traditional)/Desserts
DRINKS: No Booze
SERVING: Breakfast, Lunch & Dinner
PRICE RANGE: $$
NEIGHBORHOOD: Eastside
Very absorbing space located in an old warehouse that seems a combination of restaurant, meat store, craft store and gift shop. Here you'll also find baked goods, specialty foods, cheeses, beer and wine. Great choice for Sunday Brunch. Dine-in or take-out. Great fun just to browse.

MUSE RESTAURANT AND WINE BAR
82 Society St., 843-577-1102
www.charlestonmuse.com
CUISINE: American, Italian, Mediterranean
DRINKS: Full bar
SERVING: Dinner daily
PRICE RANGE: $$$

There are 100 wine offerings by the glass and 500 bottle offerings from producers all around the world, who create products that are true to their region, history, and varietal. The menu offers dishes inspired by the many cultures of the Mediterranean and is prepared with local ingredients.

NANA'S SEAFOOD & SOUL
176 Line St, Charleston, 843-937-0002
www.nanasseafoodsoul.com
CUISINE: Soul Food
DRINKS: No Booze
SERVING: Lunch & Dinner (close early)
PRICE RANGE: $$
NEIGHBORHOOD: Jonestown
Small eatery known for its menu of authentic soul food. Specials change daily but the chef utilizes local ingredients including the seafood, which is why you can only get shrimp & grits when they have freshly

caught shrimp. Speaking of shrimp, you're going to love their shrimp: after being perfectly cooked, the shrimp are slathered with a brown sauce made of yellow, red and orange peppers, sausage and bacon. Also tops are the deviled crabs and the "chewies," brownies stuffed with pecans. They only have 3 tables, so this is mostly a take-out place.

THE OBSTINATE DAUGHTER
2063 Middle St, Sullivan's Island, 843-416-5020
www.theobstinatedaughter.com
CUISINE: Pizza, Seafood, Mediterranean
DRINKS: Full Bar
SERVING: Lunch & Dinner

PRICE RANGE: $$
NEIGHBORHOOD: Sullivan's Island
A chic rustic eatery that pays homage to the rich history of Sullivan's Island, the walls are made with gorgeous reclaimed wood with loads of texture and charm. Menu features a nice mixture of seafood and Mediterranean dishes. Favorites include: Frogmore Chowder and Bucatini Carbonara. The pizzas from the wood-fired ovens are made with flour from heritage-grain champ Anson Mills. Nice desserts like their N.C. apple bread pudding and red velvet cake.

THE ORDINARY
544 King St, Charleston, 843-414-7060

www.eattheordinary.com
CUISINE: Seafood, Sandwiches; Southern
DRINKS: Full Bar
SERVING: Dinner
PRICE RANGE: $$$
Set in an old bank building from 1927, this spot has a striking décor with high ceilings and large arched windows. By the old bank vault you'll see the big raw bar stacked high with clams, oysters and crabs. (Try the pickled shrimp.) Labeled as an American brasserie and Oyster Hall, this eatery offers Chef Mike Lata's take on Southern seafood. Menu favorites include: Lobster Roll, swordfish schnitzel, Black Bass Provencal, and Peekytoe Crab Louie. Best experience is to share lots of small plates. Desserts offered include the delicious Carolina Rice Pudding with Peaches and Figs.

PEARLZ OYSTER BAR
153 East Bay St, Charleston, 843-577-5755
www.pearlzoysterbar.com
CUISINE: Seafood
DRINKS: Full Bar
SERVING: Dinner
PRICE RANGE: $$
Located in the heart of the historic district, this eclectic seafood eatery is a great way to experience Charleston. Menu favorites include: Blackened Mahi Mahi over cheddar grits and Tuna Tartar. Creative desserts. No reservations. Sometimes a wait.

PENINSULA GRILL
Planter's Inn

112 N Market St, Charleston, 843-723-0700
www.peninsulagrill.com
CUISINE: American (New)/Steakhouse
DRINKS: Full Bar
SERVING: Dinner nightly
PRICE RANGE: $$$$

When you stroll up the red brick walkway
meandering through a lushly landscape courtyard,
you know you're in for something special. Posh
eatery (velvet walls) with a creative menu of upscale
Southern fare. A recent starter I loved was Lobster
Skillet Cake & Crab Cake Duo with Smoked Bacon-
Parsley Salad and Creamed Corn. I followed it with

pan-seared Carolina trout with blue crab and capers. (Menu is seasonal, so it changes.) Where else can you get a slice of coconut cake that's 12 layers high? This cake is so famous they will even ship it to you by overnight express (for $130). I admit I never tasted it. (I always get the orange vanilla cheesecake.) Insist on a table outside in the courtyard if the weather suits.

POOGAN'S PORCH RESTAURANT
72 Queen St., 843-577-2337
www.poogansporch.com
CUISINE: Southern
DRINKS: Full bar

SERVING: Lunch and dinner daily, brunch Sat - Sun
PRICE RANGE: $$

Tucked away on charming Queen Street, Poogan's Porch is one of Charleston's oldest independent culinary establishments, with a fresh approach to Lowcountry cuisine. Recognized by Martha Stewart Living, Wine Spectator and The Travel Channel, this beautifully restored Victorian house is the perfect southern spot for lunch, dinner or weekend brunch. Since opening in 1976, Poogan's Porch has been a favorite of well-known celebrities, politicians, tourists and locals alike who rave about this Southern institution. Whether it's a warm homemade buttermilk biscuit and sausage gravy for brunch, a bowl of she-crab soup for lunch, or our signature buttermilk fried chicken for dinner, your meal at Poogan's will be unforgettable. A state-of-the-art, 1500-bottle wine cellar and over 28 wines offered by the glass will be a perfect complement to any meal.

PURLIEU

237 Fishburne St, 843-300-2253
www.purlieucharleston.com
CUISINE: French
DRINKS: Wine Bar
SERVING: Dinner, Closed Sun & Mon.
PRICE RANGE: $$$
NEIGHBORHOOD: Westside

Casual bistro atmosphere enhanced by the slated wood ceiling gives this French place a welcoming feel. Small, and even cramped when it gets busy, but that's not a negative. I liked it that way. They have a creative menu featuring bouillabaisse, duck prosciutto

& fusion French cuisine. Favorites: Hanger Steak and Frog Legs with puff pastry. Save room for the 100-layer Chocolate cake. Reservations recommended.

RENZO
384 Huger St, 843-259-2760
www.renzochs.com
CUISINE: Pizza, Italian
DRINKS: Wine Bar
SERVING: Dinner, Lunch & Dinner on Sundays, Closed Mondays
PRICE RANGE: $$$
NEIGHBORHOOD: Downtown
Popular upscale eatery in a long narrow room with a friendly bar on one side complemented with booths against the other wall – they have really tasty wood-fired Neapolitan pizza—a large selection, like and Wrath of Kahan pizza (piquillo pepper sauce, chorizo, medjool dates) and other fare, like Wood-fired Eggplant and Lo Mein Carbonara. Extensive wine list.

RITA'S SEASIDE GRILLE
2 Center St, Folly Beach, 843-588-2525
www.ritasseasidegrille.com
CUISINE: Burgers/Seafood
DRINKS: Full Bar
SERVING: Breakfast, Lunch & Dinner
PRICE RANGE: $$
NEIGHBORHOOD: Folly Beach
A fun spot located just steps from the beach and the Folly Fishing Pier. Menu is typical American fare of

burgers and seafood. Favorites include the award-winning Rita's Chili.

RODNEY SCOTT'S BBQ
1011 King St, 843-990-9535
www.rodneyscottsbbq.com
CUISINE: Barbecue
DRINKS: Full Bar
SERVING: Lunch & Dinner
PRICE RANGE: $$
NEIGHBORHOOD: North Central
Popular counter-serve eatery offering Low Country-style smoked pulled pork BBQ, chicken and ribs. Has a big to-go business, but there are a few booths and other tables if you want to eat here. Outside, they have some picnic tables where you can also eat, with the wood they use to smoke their meats stacked high between the tables. Favorites: Southern-fried catfish and Smoked Turkey.

THE ROOFTOP
19 Vendue Range, Charleston, 843-414-2337
www.thevendue.com/charleston-dining/the-rooftop
CUISINE: American (Traditional)/Lounge
DRINKS: Full Bar
SERVING: Lunch & Dinner
PRICE RANGE: $$
NEIGHBORHOOD: French Quarter
Located on the rooftop of the **Vendue Hotel**, this place is great as a meeting spot for lunch. From this vantage point you get a great view of the church steeples that puncture the city's skyline, as well a super good view of the harbor. Excellent at happy

hour for a sunset you'll remember. Favorites: Pulled Pork Nachos and Signature Lobster Rolls. Extensive cocktail menu. Great views.

RUTLEDGE CAB CO
1300 Rutledge Ave, Charleston, 843-720-1440
www.rutledgecabco.com
CUISINE: American (New), Burgers
DRINKS: Full Bar
SERVING: Lunch & Dinner
PRICE RANGE: $$
Located in a former convenience store/gas station, this popular eatery offers a menu of American comfort food. Many of the menu favorites are cooked over Charleston's only indoor charcoal grill. Indoor and outdoor seating.

SECOND STATE COFFEE
70 1/2 Beaufain St, Charleston, 843-793-4402
https://secondstatecoffee.com
CUISINE: Coffee & Tea
DRINKS: Full Bar

SERVING: 7 a.m. – 7 p.m.
PRICE RANGE: $$
A minimalist coffee bar that offers coffees,
beverages, and a variety of pastries.
Free Wi-Fi.

THE SHELLMORE
357 N Shelmore Blvd, 843-654-9278
www.theshellmore.com
CUISINE: Seafood
DRINKS: Wine Bar
SERVING: Dinner, Closed Sun & Mon.
NEIGHBORHOOD: Mount Pleasant
Cozy eatery featuring a wine and raw bar, which is
why I come here—the OYSTERS, which are among
the plumpest, juiciest I've had in Charleston. There is
big horseshoe-shaped bar inside and some pleasant
outdoor seating as well. Menu changes daily – mostly
sandwiches and small plates. Favorites: Charred
octopus; Country Paté, Beef & Pork Ragu over
capunti pasta.

STARS ROOFTOP & GRILL ROOM
495 King St, Charleston, 843-577-0100
www.starsrestaurant.com
CUISINE: American/Steakhouse
DRINKS: Full Bar
SERVING: Dinner nightly, Lunch on weekends
PRICE RANGE: $$$
Located in the historic district, this stunning 1930's style Grill Room and Walnut Bar offers a seasonal menu of steaks and regional dishes – shared and large places. Menu favorites include: Grass fed NC Bone-in Rib eye and Lobster & Grits. For a treat reserve a seat at the Chef's Table (seats 12) for a top-notch dining experience.

THE SWAMP FOX
Francis Marion Hotel
387 King St, Charleston, 843-724-8888
www.francismarionhotel.com/
CUISINE: American (New)/Southern
DRINKS: Full Bar

SERVING: Breakfast, Lunch & Dinner
PRICE RANGE: $$
Located in the historic Francis Marion Hotel, this popular eatery (originally opened in 1924) offers a revolving menu of regional specialties inspired by the Old South. Award-wining shrimp & grits served with a white lobster-based gravy and topped off with orange peppers, scallions and bits of smoked Tasso ham. The grits themselves come from an historic Columbia mill named Adluh. (Get the appetizer portion instead of the main course just so you can taste this great dish.) Live jazz piano on weekends.

TACO BOY
217 Huger St, Charleston, 843-789-3333
www.tacoboy.net
CUISINE: Mexican
DRINKS: Full Bar
SERVING: Lunch & Dinner
PRICE RANGE: $$
An authentic Taqueria/Cantina that offers a creative
menu of Mexican fare featuring tacos with innovative
fillings. Great frozen cocktails. Indoor and outdoor
seating.

TATTOOED MOOSE
1137 Morrison Dr, 843-277-2990
www.tattooedmoose.com
CUISINE: American Traditional
DRINKS: Full Bar
SERVING: Lunch & Dinner

PRICE RANGE: $$
NEIGHBORHOOD: Downtown
Popular neighborhood spot serving upscale bar food
& sandwiches. There's a big dead moose head
hanging over the bar, so hunters will feel especially
welcome. Lots of other dead critters, like a beaver, or
parts of dead critters, a couple of antlers, a cow's
skull, decorating the walls. Graffiti is everywhere,
and I mean everywhere. It's your dream idea of a dive
bar atmosphere. A couple of pinball machines. A
favorite is the Duck Club served with Duck fat fries.
Lots of other very tasty bar grub. Craft beers.

VIRGINIA'S ON KING

412 King St, Charleston, 843-735-5800
www.holycityhospitality.com/virginias-on-king
CUISINE: Southern
DRINKS: Beer & Wine Only
SERVING: Breakfast, Lunch & Dinner
PRICE RANGE: $$
This upscale favorite is known for its Southern
comfort food dishes made from old family recipes
(even their fried pickles). Menu favorites include:
blackened catfish, fried chicken, she-crab soup and
the Lowcountry Boil, a hearty stew containing
sausage, potatoes, corn and shrimp. Their key lime
pie is a standout.

WILD OLIVE RESTAURANT
2867 Maybank Hwy, Johns Island, 843-737-4177
www.wildoliverestaurant.com
CUISINE: Italian
DRINKS: Full Bar
SERVING: Lunch & Dinner
PRICE RANGE: $$
NEIGHBORHOOD: John's Island
A friendly eatery with a rustic-chic vibe that offers a simple menu of Italian fare. Portions are large and the food is good. Favorites include: Short Ribs and Calamari Napoletano. Nice wine list. First certified green restaurant in S.C.

WORKMEN'S CAFÉ
1837 N Grimball Rd, 843-406-0120
No Website
CUISINE: Seafood / Soul Food / Southern
DRINKS: No Booze
SERVING: Lunch 11-4 (till 6 on Fri); Closed Sat, Sun & Mon.

PRICE RANGE: $
NEIGHBORHOOD: James Island
Very, very reasonably-priced cafeteria style eatery serving seafood, soul food and Southern specialties. Favorites: Pork chops; Country fried steak; Okra; Red rice, BBQ. Damn, it's ALL good.

WRECK OF THE RICHARD & CHARLENE
106 Haddrell St, 843-884-0052
www.wreckrc.com
DRINKS: Beer & Wine
SERVING: Dinner from 5, but closed Monday
PRICE RANGE: $$
NEIGHBORHOOD: Mount Pleasant
Simple eatery that has to be one of the most picturesque you'll find anywhere, as it overlooks a working marina. Sit outside (or inside) and look out over some real working fishing boats and saltwater marshes. There are still some wetlands wading birds that show up. Get a look at this scene now—it won't be here forever. This is a locals' favorite serving Low Country-style fried seafood. What I love about this place is that there are no concessions to "landlubbers." The food here is strictly seafood, and most of that is fried, fried, fried. (But you can still get broiled and grilled items.) Favorites: Grilled scallops; Fried oysters, Deviled crab and definitely the Hush puppies. Just get the Seafood Platter and be done with it. Paper plates and menus here. Just circle your choice with a red marker. Desserts are homemade, and my favorite is the Key Lime Bread Pudding. No reservations, no a/c (a screened in porch), no cell

phone use in dining room (you have to go outside). Good for them! At least they take credit cards, LOL.

XIAO BAO BISCUIT
224 Rutledge Ave, Charleston, No Phone
www.xiaobaobiscuit.com
CUISINE: Vietnamese, Japanese, Taiwanese
DRINKS: Full Bar
SERVING: Lunch & Dinner daily; closed Sunday
PRICE RANGE: $$$
Located in a converted gas station, this trendy multicultural eatery offers a menu of Asian comfort food. Vegan/Vegetarian/Gluten-free options available. Specialty cocktails.

ZERO RESTAURANT + BAR
0 George St, 843-817-7900
www.zerogeorge.com - for hotel
https://zerorestaurantcharleston.com/ - for restaurant
CUISINE: American (New)
DRINKS: Full Bar
SERVING: Dinner, Closed Mondays
PRICE RANGE: $$$
NEIGHBORHOOD: East Side, NoMo
Located in the restored 1804 **Zero George Street Hotel**, this unique café offers award-winning cuisine in a very Colonial setting within the hotel that's made up on 3 historic houses and a courtyard. Very elegant, very romantic, very charming. It's nice to slip in to have a drink at the tiny little bar or sit out on the verandah. There's a chef's tasting menu available, and this changes all the time, so not sure wht you'll get the night you visit. Favorites: Beef Wellington

and Scallop Tartare. Vegetarian options available. Classic cocktails. There's also a happy hour and a small Bar Menu (things like Lobster Rolls, Deviled Eggs, Charcuterie Board).

NIGHTLIFE

Charleston is not particularly known for its night life
— the options sometimes come down to one
outlandishly named martini versus another (caramel
macchiatotini? Charlestoniantini?). But locals with an
evening to kill stop by the lounge of their choice.

BIN 152
152 King St, Charleston, 843-577-7359
www.bin152.com
Bin 152 is known as Charleston's best wine bar (with
hints of France in its décor of marble-topped café
tables and wainscoting, but there are communal tables
also), but it's also a cheese bar, art gallery and

antiques market. Located in the French Quarter, BIN 152 offers 30 different wines by the glass and over 130 wines by the bottle. They serve over 40 different cheeses and charcuteries with freshly baked bread.

COCKTAIL CLUB
479 King St #200, Charleston, 843-724-9411
www.thecocktailclubcharleston.com/
Located above **The Macintosh**, this upscale lounge celebrates the craft cocktail. If you're into creative cocktails stop here and sample one of their house-made infusions or rare liquors. Three lounge areas including a rooftop terrace and custom garden. Menu of light fare available. Live music.

THE GIN JOINT
182 E Bay St, Charleston, 843-577-6111
www.theginjoint.com
The Gin Joint serves quality pre-prohibition style cocktails made from locally sourced herbs, house made syrups, and top tier booze. Great drink menu and wonderful soft pretzels.

THE GRIFFON
18 Vendue Range St, Charleston, 843-723-1700
www.griffoncharleston.com
This English Pub was voted "Best Bar in the South" by *Southern Living*. Located in the historic district, this popular hangout offers local brews on tap, several TVs, and friendly staff.

MYNT
135 Calhoun St, Charleston, 843-718-1598
www.myntcharleston.com

Mynt is a popular new bar/club with a great innovative design catering to the young professionals. Mynt offers great variety of cocktails and appetizers. Weekends are busy so be prepared to wait in line.

PAVILION BAR AT THE MARKET PAVILION HOTEL
225 E Bay St, Charleston, 843-723-0500
www.marketpavilion.com/pavilionbar.cfm
This place makes a perfect stop for a nightcap before turning in. From the rooftop bar you can look out over the church steeples and into the waters of the Ashley river pulsing by. Off to your north you'll see the lighted Ravenel Bridge soaring over the U.S.S. Yorktown Museum.

INDEX

71

WRECK OF THE RICHARD & CHARLENE, 60

Lightning Source UK Ltd.
Milton Keynes UK
UKHW022226041222
413345UK00011B/1609